Next to Everything that is Breakable

by

Kara Knickerbocker

Finishing Line Press
Georgetown, Kentucky

Next to Everything that is Breakable

ACKNOWLEDGMENTS

Heartfelt thanks to the following publications where some of the poems in this book first
appeared, sometimes in different versions and/or with different titles:

Amaryllis: "Remember When"
Avatar Review: "The Foundation," "Afterbirth," "Burning," "Road Maps," "Oceans of Her
Own"
Broad River Review: "Sixteen"
Construction Magazine: "Salt"
Eunoia Review: "Made with Love," "Say It," "Last Night Awake in Bed"
Moledro Magazine: "They Told Me," "Beating"
Pittsburgh City Paper: "All Safeties Off"
Pittsburgh Poetry Review: "Tuesday at Baum Grove," "If You're Asking Why I'm Leaving"
Rat's Ass Review: "Spring Beast," "Sex in the Bedroom of a Childhood Home"
Uppagus: "Portrait of Your Grandfather, Dying"
VerseWrights: "A Dying Art," "French Creek Water Trail," "Where I Want to Belong,"
"Passport"
Voices from the Attic, Vol. XXII: "Saved," "Formula"

Publisher: Leah Maines

Editor: Christen Kincaid

Cover Art: Catherine Frisina

Author Photo: Lauren Demby, www.LaurenReneeDesigns.com

Cover Design: Debra Vieira

Printed in the USA on acid-free paper.
Order online: www.finishinglinepress.com
also available on amazon.com

Author inquiries and mail orders:
Finishing Line Press
P. O. Box 1626
Georgetown, Kentucky 40324
U. S. A.

Contents

To my parents, for giving me this world
& letting me split it wide open
and to J.J., for showing me how to
fiercely love all its brokenness

PART ONE

Spring Beast

Blackberried and full,
I caught the last flight out of Charleston.

I dreaded the slush up north, the way
my eyes understood goodbye.
So I hunkered for hours
in the airport bar,
fingering long neck bottles of beer
with my index finger
(like you did my throat).

I tried to construct poetry
from another man's facial features
just to see if I could.
(I can't.)

Leaving never bothered me
when I knew how to write the next line.
But I am greeting April with no words—
only whiskey doubles,
the naked itch to taste you still.

I am going back to Pittsburgh alone
to starve on the altar of a twin size mattress,
to see the face of a dog in my dreams.

All Safeties Off

It was Christmas Day in our backyard
when I first shot my dad's hunting rifle—
felt it kick back into my shoulder
as he looked on,
keeping distance
as shells went flying.

I fingered the trigger,
breathed the weight of it all—
burning hot metal
swallowing painted targets,
my shaky hands steadying & aiming—
all safeties off.

& I thought,
here I am
deep in December—sweating
because
there was something
within the chamber
I couldn't point to
barreling through me
just the same
& the weapon clicks
white knuckle grip.

I need to reload, but what's the point
if all my ghosts wear bulletproof vests
& don't understand the word *no*
or *stop*
& my dad yells, *Bull's eye!*

& I drop
the gun.

Saved

They believed
there was a science
to the way it happened,
ash skin fading
fast to blue
in the bathroom light.

My arms locked up,
rigid as the walls
separating left and right brain
unable to see with rolled back eyes
you, sweating there on the hemisphere.

They admired
how I hit the floor with such precision.
What a flawless dance, and it was—
narrowly missing my cerebellum,
limbs crumpled like tissue paper.
Beautiful and dead weight.

They were amazed
at the way my pulse played hide and seek
then how the flow of blood back into my brain
washed realization over you:
squeezing my hands,
kissing impossible breaths into my lungs,
compressing what you couldn't fathom in your hands.
A savior over science.

They said the tests were inconclusive—
It is unexplainable.
I said, *Put all your bets on theories*
Prove your faith in God
and they couldn't speak.

They Told Me

Don't take taxis from outside the Lima airport.
Danger's written on the license plate, theft will snatch you
quicker than you can pray to Pachamama.
There are men always hungry for something more
they said—*book a cab from inside.*

So I did.

Late 40s, thick Spanish tongue, leathered skin,
he let out an odd laugh at the sight of my hiking boots.
You can sit up front, he motioned
as I climbed into the backseat, the weight of my pack now a comfort.
Fragments of language flew as we talked *Cusco, ceviche, cervezas.*
I gripped the door handle close as he scanned me in the rearview,
said, *Muy bonita. Me gusta mucho*…spun
around, slid a hand fast up my thigh—
split me in a place I can't tell you

Beating
-after Diane Glancy

If they would have prescribed an easier pill to swallow than news
that this device was necessary to keep me breathing—

If they could have explained the eternity in 20 seconds of a heartbeat
    stopping—

If they could have warned me that the first time wouldn't work and
    anesthesia would deliver me
to the table again before seeing my family—

If they could have prepared my mother before she saw my adult body
    naked in a tub
or me before feeling her hands help bathe, dress me—

If they could have just said never mind wearing a strapless wedding
    dress—

If they could have written in the reports how wonderful it is that
    you're a runner
but you should probably find a new hobby now—

If they could have diagnosed the symptoms of their words, "It's a
    shame, you're so young"—

If they would have just realized more than this caged organ beats like
    hell inside me

If they would have just defined *pacemaker* as a parasite in a body I
    used to know.

Tuesday at Baum Grove

I am barefoot, sitting cross-legged in that park behind Aldi's,
picking off dry skin on the soles of my feet.
You are on speaker phone, telling me how to cook zucchini
and wondering if I thought about moving in with my boyfriend yet.

I tell you about the armed robbery last night off Fifth Ave,
how two of my burners don't work,
and try to figure out how to dig the lump out of my throat.

I still remember when he told me, "Loving you is a chore."

I swish amber ale on top of my tongue
wondering where things went wrong,
if anyone would be up for the job.

Passport

I will forget textbook Alps
until I jump from the top of them.
I will trip over my own two feet
trying to learn Flamenco,
drinking sangria in southern Spain
as the sun settles on my shoulders
for company.

I will ride a camel in Morocco, feel
exposed in my own skin when men's eyes
chisel through my dress. I will cry
on my 23rd birthday, sitting alone
on the Mediterranean shore.
I will meet men who lie to me in *discotecas*
and on long distance flights.

I will see my mother only through a screen,
try to touch anything but the empty space.
I will create a new sense of home
still five thousand miles away
from the only one I've ever known.

I will believe things are better
in Barcelona with best friends
until I wake up in empty hotel rooms.
I will become intoxicated
and invincible in Ibiza, parasailing
into raving sunsets, only to swallow
regret with a rising headache.

In Paris I will wish I locked my own love,
eat dinner atop the Eiffel Tower
as French fashion seeps into my suitcase.
I will befriend strangers in Belgium,
under bright lights and the mist after rainfall.
I will love how it feels to binge
on chocolate and beer I can't pronounce.

In Switzerland I will stand on Schilthorn
and know there is a God. I will linger
in blues and greens until my pupils
are delirious in happiness, my wet
eyelashes sick at the thought of departure.

I will reign in Prague as I map the bridges
by hand and bury a castle of beautiful fists.
In Venice I will crave gelato
like I did your affection, cling
to a brother I have not seen in years
only to fight with him through Old Town,
with Mozart composing at our backs.

I will photograph the light of Budapest
from the Opera House steps, and not really understand
how to belong. In Germany I will puff my breasts
with dirndl dress and anchor my stomach
with bratwurst. I will have to use both hands
to hold a stein to my lips, pass out
from foreign words.

And in six months when I return
to America, I won't know who I am or where
I belong because I am inked like stamps
on a passport, tainted with the taste of *tapas*,
charging like a train that never stops.

The Foundation

We were shelving time until one of us
could gather up the money or guts to say it,
and you framed a place where we almost
made love,
carried us up steps to assemble
a right way to start this.

I laid the foundation right there myself
on that cream carpet in your father's house
leaving a hinged mouth to the May night
as if to welcome
the idea of us beginning.

We were tracking months of blueprints,
hoping they would measure up,
and you said you would keep the light on
and build,
so long as I wrote.

PART TWO

Salt

I will eat *paella* and *pan con tomate* until I die, if you want me to—
salt clawing and clutching the corners of my mouth
like your newborn child's tiny hands around her mother's finger.

But we don't speak about it in the kitchen. We let infidelity churn
in wedding pots and knead curved skin like bread dough.

We savor a kiss; you feed it to me in spoonfuls, in haste
and wipe the edges neatly with your napkin before you go.

Your apron is burned in the morning. I do not ask why.

Say It

When a child asks, *What is love?*
Describe it as a sunburn—
From the first glow, to stomach sky
like you've swallowed the sun whole.
Bronzed, still basking in warmth.

       Explain passion as hot hot heat.
       Tell of the love that sears
       through layer after delicate layer.
       Learn from the blisters.

              Just say how important it is
              to still know your own skin below
              when it all peels away.

If You're Asking Why I'm Leaving

Because this row of brick houses ghosts with heads on backwards,
because my skin sleeps under your nailbeds,
because there isn't a color red I've loved since the car crash.

Because even birds fly south
because without wings, your lips travel down just the same
because I let you,
because religion was the well-oiled machine of our bodies.

Because thoughts of a baby's open mouth,
because I am egg yolk,
because I cannot imagine anything more breakable than if I stay.

Remember When

I caught salamanders from the pond beside our house—
counted twenty orange speckled bodies
inside the glass bowl I stole from the kitchen.

Remember how they gripped sides of their new home
for a way out
only to slide down, plop
on top of each other

I put flat rocks & leaves at the bottom,
made it home—
remember how much I loved that they couldn't escape
(unless I let them)

I wanted so badly to keep them,
snuck the bowl upstairs to your bedroom—
I can't remember where you were
but I was there, careful to listen
for creaks of floorboards/ the weight of someone
sure to find me

They climbed across the plains of my open palms,
pawed at the air when held up from the tail
and in the slow blink of a golden eye
maybe I knew it was wrong
so I kissed closed mouths—
remember their still-wet webbed feet
made me feel like a mother?

Remember I didn't know what salamanders ate
pushed the bowl far under your bed when called for dinner
never washed my hands of their spots—
forgot after school the next day

Remember the slap of stench in the morning,
murky with fresh death—
remember the look on my face when
mother said she was missing a bowl?

Sixteen

Slow, now
before embers of Newports burn
out like leaving the body unchained,
before being baptized in wet cement
next to everything that is breakable.

Quick, now
after drinking dusk with windows down,
after crossing bridges built by new tongues
while we still taste a summer
that is not yet ours.

Siempre

I don't know what I'll find there on the shore, *amor*
space for me to breathe in salt water
as sea creatures crawl from point A to B—
the only cultured dance I know.

And in it, my hips will give *besos* to dark haired men
who scan them under thick eyebrows
like the old Spanish arches
I will soon stand beneath.

Maybe pureness is what I am searching for
in the eyes of *los niños*,
or making this body my home—
all my stationery can't be sure.

I could only taste the bland rice of my life,
long for the fire of a different sun,
for *comida* to burn my lips
and leave my stomach never the same.

I asked *mi madre* if love did that.
She just smiled and shook her head,
told me *la casa* is where
I would unpack my bags and stay
forever and *siempre.*

Road Maps

pull through the backs of my wrists
when he asks me what's wrong.
I choke on the other line,
oceans between us
and think about home,
about my jealous bones,
about kids and the military,
things I've seen from this side of the sun.

I consider telling him a lot has changed—
that I stopped feeling something when he sang along
to the radio. But I say nothing, and know somehow
we won't be looking at rings anymore.

Formula

I have found there is no straight line to the surface,
no borders to keep the hunger at bay when it crawls
home into bed with me,
and no way to find a solution to infinity.

Still, I understand the equation.

I know the way my cells burst when you pluck me
from a field of lost,
the way you smooth my insecurities like white linen on hotel beds.

Most of all, I know the way my spine contracts and collapses,
unraveling
me at the sight of you leaving.

An Ocean of Her Own

The five-year-old face of España,
still alive in my camera memory—
her hand painted emerald eyes
daring to open and close as she sleeps.
She tiptoes at midnight
into my dreams and screams at noon
behind burgundy lips for *galletas*, for home,
and when she swims naked under a June sun,
her dark locks waterfall down
the small of her back.

I try to remember being as free.

She is God filling through the piano rods
her pillars Catalan mountains
as she shields the weather
from her younger brother.
She is beauty in the twirl of an 'r',
a thirst never quenched
by all the salt water on Earth—
an ocean of her own, kissing
the coast of her cheeks
as she stubs a toe on the edge
of the horizon
and the world
gasps.

PART THREE

Where I Want to Belong
Blanes, 2013

You always say the same thing, he told me
when I said that the view of Blanes was beautiful.
But how can you tire of a coastline
kissing the neck of its town
of the Catalan people and the pizzerias,
the *supermercats* and *gelaterias*?

I will never get used to *cava* pouring
into mouths whose voices I've come to worship,
or how the music swallows the streets,
sun spreading like butter on toast over *Sa Palomera,*
where someone is locking their love.

I cannot stop searching for constellations
I wish shared my name
that I saw through a stranger's telescope
on the rooftop of *Castell Sant Joan*
that golden Sunday night.

I am pocketing chocolate *dolços*
and little hearts in my hands
as I wave red and gold independence
above their *platges,*

homesick with the realization
that this place, right here,
is where I want to belong...
and knowing I'm never coming back.

A Dying Art

I saw paintings there I wish I hadn't—
Picasso dripping in his yellow sadness
heaving against the awning of a French silhouette
and there were Monets and van Goghs
slinking through Renaissance hallways
avoiding admission fees and knocking over oil paints.

I was busy shaking hands
with some 18th century architecture, continents
short of the last home I loved, and thinking that
sculpting a way out of this depression
was a dying art.

Afterbirth

If I had one comfort in this new home
it would be in the fetal position, with my back against
the open womb of a tub, pretending tears
were from your shampooed hands
that once held my head.

I gave birth to a dream I wasn't ready for
but you nurtured it just the same,
even as I entered that pot–bellied plane
you knew would take your baby away.

For weeks, I've daydreamed in starched sheets
missing you, my mother, and how it felt
to be under a safe moon
when setting sail was just a trip to the grocery store.

I felt the amniotic fluid stream down your cheeks
from 5,000 miles away and wished
that I could be more selfless,
that the umbilical cord was never severed.

I bought a dress yesterday with the euros
you secretly tucked in my purse.
They were fruits of your labor—
the crowning reason I breathe,

and I didn't even think to buy you a souvenir.

Sex in the Bedroom of a Childhood Home

Lips drift across clavicle bone
just breathe he whispers
but you can't—
Not with your parents sleeping
beneath these floorboards.

You've never felt your naked body
under this rose-printed quilt,
never felt this much a child.

Years ago, you learned to maneuver
your weight around the exhale of wood—
How to side step expanding cracks
sneaking upstairs at sixteen,
firewater still dancing on your tongue.

Yet now, an adult woman,
you can't pinpoint the place
where the worn mattress moans,
how sound amplifies with the telling of two bodies—
where the headboard grinds
against the willing wall
(or how hard)

All the while, he fills you—
Memories gather like glass figurines
your mother carefully placed
on the shelf
when you moved away.

Made With Love

The doctors poured deep breaths from coffee pots,
fed me through IVs.
They carved a slice in my warm bread of a body
served the scar sunny-side up,
embroidered my skin to match the napkin
they wiped their hands clean of blood and
what's left—

Hiccups and a hard, flat line,
a heart so swollen
you wonder
if the battered mess will ever rise.

Last Night Awake in Bed

and in between the rise and fall of your chest,
I pleaded the morning wouldn't wake you—
that the war wouldn't come creeping
and rip you coldly from the covers.
I know how you must have paced just the same,
all this while, waiting on me overseas
hoping I'd come back home.

I am here now beside you in the dark,
tracing the muscles in your back
and thinking of how you will sleep:
first in hotel beds, and in the backseat of trucks,
in aisle seats on airplanes, next to a stranger
who will become like your brother
on a stiff cot set on foreign ground.

Your brown sugar eyes will drift and see slideshows
in bullets— gunfire only God knows. Even if I hand-
wrote it in letters and cut through crossfire
they wouldn't know: how your shallow breaths
come in threes as you doze, or
your feet that twitch just on the cusp of sinking.
And they don't care if you wake.

They will count you like numbered sheep.

And as you'll be lacing your boots for another day,
I will toss in the currents of an uncertain slumber
with a dial tone sleeping against my ear.
No heat of a body cradling my backbone,
no awkward arm or hot breath on my neck,
just hair-raised skin drenched from the soldiered
sweat of a distant dream, trying to find
a way back home.

Portrait of Your Grandfather, Dying

We will label it kidney failure or lung disease,
but feel the swelling notion that he
is not leaving us, but joining her—

whose ashes answer his prayers at night from the bedside table
where he props his cane,
who framed the corner of his lips with the word "happy,"
who gently takes the paintbrush and colors him home.

He raged with war,
he created love.
He is ripe for heaven.
Can you see it?

French Creek Water Trail

Sometimes they surge through telephone wires
or drip
from the kitchen faucet my father couldn't fix.
Memories of home are always moving—
streaming hot fudge down Dairy Isle sundaes after soccer
practice,
sweat and sweet meeting for the first time.

Or the pouring, moments after my mom says, "It's gonna rain—
look at the cows laying down,"
cruising by a farm past highway 98
in a Chevy that still runs
like the effortless flow of gossip in a one stoplight town.
Population: 997.

They trickle
into my nostrils:
trace of wood chips,
gasoline, the flood
of burnt blackberry pancakes for breakfast.
Sometimes they spill over, tears down cheeks
after a punch from my older brother.

But the swiftest circuit in Saegertown is French Creek,
the blue vein that never runs off course.
The one that separates the school from the Dairy Isle,
the one that George Washington sailed in 1753.

My father told me never to swim there—
his classmate drowned
the Friday after high school graduation
in an inner tube, among friends,
swallowed by a strong undercurrent.
Population: 996.

The boy's mother still left the porch light on,
every night for thirty years
until she got swept away, too.
That's why the river is muddied, not blue or forgiving.

It is clouded with the bodies of a twelve-year-old girl
whose canoe buckled in June
and a six-year-old boy, ever curious
that toppled into a whirlpool.
995. 994. 993.

All were carried away
as my mother will be, and my father,
my brother (though he'll put up one hell of a fight)
and someday, me, even with
grass safe beneath my feet.

Whiskey Kiss

This is when you feel it,
from shards of Jack bottles in temples
to finger, and fuck, and forgetting—
our bellies like a sponge on the ocean floor.

Destitute with adoration,
we are incapable and ugly,
crawling home,
leaving the door wide open.

Notes

"Beating" takes inspiration from Diane Glancy's "Those Old Voices Always Are With Me."

"The Foundation" is for J.J. Yamnitzky.

"An Ocean of Her Own" is for Mar Alum.

"Where I Want to Belong" was written in Blanes, Girona, Spain.

"Afterbirth" is for LuAnn Knickerbocker.

"Portrait of Your Grandfather, Dying" is in memory of Vincent Siragusa.

"French Creek Water Trail" takes inspiration from the tributary in Northwestern Pennsylvania and is for Dan Knickerbocker.

Additional Acknowledgements

This book would not have been possible without the help of many selfless individuals.

Thank you: to my remarkable teachers, especially Jan Beatty, Nancy Kirkwood, Bill and Stacey Hetrick, for instilling in me the love for words and all they can do; to my brilliant mentor, Tess Barry, for committed guidance and deep trust; to Jennifer Jackson Berry, Jen Ashburn, Alyse Richmond, and Laurin Wolf for their infinite patience and inspiration; to Michael Albright and Dan Shapiro for endless encouragement; to the Madwomen in the Attic, every single one, for mad love and mad support; to Catherine Frisina and Debra Vieira for their talents and vision with the cover design; to all my wonderful friends and family for their continuous belief in me; to the family and home I made in Blanes and around the globe— these poems are because of all of you; to my loving parents Dan and LuAnn Knickerbocker for their sacrifices and unconditional love; and to my entire heart, J.J. Yamnitzky. I love you. And, of course, to Finishing Line Press for the birth of this dream.